Adelma Grenier Simmons

A Year in Wreaths

Caprilands' Guide to Wreaths

Photographed by George Gregory Wieser

For Leslie on her 33rd
birthday.

Love,
Mom

MALLARD
PRESS

MALLARD PRESS
An Imprint of BDD Promotional Book Company, Inc.
666 Fifth Avenue
New York, NY 10103

This book is meant to be educational in nature and is in no way meant to be used for self-treatment or self-diagnosis. Keep in mind that excess quantities of some herbs can be dangerous. The editors have attempted to include, wherever appropriate, cautions and guidelines for using the herbs and herbal recipes in the book. Yet, we realize that it is impossible for us to anticipate every conceivable use of herbs and every possible problem any use could cause. Moreover, we cannot know just what kinds of physical reactions or allergies some of you might have to substances discussed in this book.

For this reason, Mallard Press cannot assume responsibility for the effects of using the herbs or other information in this book. And we urge that all potentially serious health problems be managed by a physician.

Table of Contents

Wreaths Through the Ages

In all eras there has been the longing for a return to simpler times, nostalgia for the basic, the natural, the homely virtues, the simplicity of the past. Never has this been more prevalent than in our complicated, modern world.

Wreath making is one of the ways we can return to a time when life was far more influenced by the seasons of the growing year, the bounty of the harvest, and the simple courses of nature.

Wreath making, throughout history, has been a way to celebrate the stirring of the seasons, and to mark holidays of personal, national or religious significance. To the ancient Greeks, wreaths were crowns of glory to signify victory, or wisdom. In the Middle Ages, wreaths marked saint's days and high church holidays. In agricultural communities, herbal wreaths expressed gratitude for the harvest, and hope for future bounty. Today, as in the past, wreaths, and the herbs of which they are composed, can enrich our appreciation of life.

St. Anthony's Nut

Celebrated on January 17, this festival, falling in mid-winter, was often celebrated with a feast of the meat salted earlier in the autumn. Meals may have included pork, as St. Anthony was the patron saint of pigs. The herb normally associated with St. Anthony is the Pignut, but as in most cold weather celebrations, fragrant herbs of all kind were employed in the decorations of the day.

Fragrance Wreath

Fragrant herbs such as rosemary, lavender, mint, lemon balm and sweet woodruff can be used either by themselves in elegant and fragrant wreaths, or placed in sweet bags of   potpourri and attached to ornamental wreaths. Combine leaves from several lemon-scented plants into an attractive wreath or make a rosemary wreath that is fragrant and useful to the gourmet cook.

St. Dorothy's Day

The Feast of St. Dorothy is celebrated on February 6 and is associated with roses. Although normally a flower of midsummer, traditionally on St. Dorothy's day brides and other celebrants were crowned with dried rose chaplets, and pelted with rose petals. In some gatherings, showers of roses were a part of the celebration.

Rose Wreath

Rosebuds, which have been dried on a tray in a well ventilated and shaded environment, can be wired into a base of silver king or sweet annie, for a lacy look. Ribbons can also be tied into the base for an attractive and colorful accent.

Whitsunday

Whitsunday or Whit-Monday is the first of the spring festivals. In agricultural communities of the past, it was the time to gather the first blossoms of spring into the house, and express hope for a bountiful growing season. Green birch trees were often cut and carried in parades by Jack of the Green, who was thought to bestow blessings of the harvest. Lilies, birch and sweet woodruff were associated with this feast day.

Lily garland

Daffodils or other spring lilies, ferns and fragrant herbs such as sweet woodruff, may be bound into a long flower rope to adorn hallways or woven into chaplets which may be worn on the head in celebration of the coming spring and to welcome the blessing of the Jack of the Green.

Green George's Day

An early spring holiday falling on April 23. The feast of Green George is an ancient Slav festival. In the past, willow trees were cut down and adorned with wreaths, flowers and garlands. Children went from door to door collecting gifts and it was believed that if householders did not give freely, their crops would not grow. Green leaves were associated with this holiday, anticipating the good things to come from the earth.

Kitchen wreath

Kitchen wreaths can be made from culinary herbs which, as they dry, can be removed and used to season foods. Thyme is a good base because it is easy to grow, abundant, and its sweetness lasts long after it has dried. Rosemary, sage, savory, dill and parsley are also good ingredients for a kitchen wreath. Wreaths can be decorated with the edible blossoms of the pot marigold. Kitchen wreaths can also be arranged bound dill stalks.

May Day

May Day, which during the Middle Ages and the Renaissance fell on May 12, is another celebration of the arrival of Spring. In medieval English villages, it was at last warm enough to spend the night in the woods, and young men and women would return in the morning bearing boughs and branches to deck the Maypole. Often a King and Queen were chosen, and adorned with the white blossoms associated with the season, hawthorne, lily of the valley, and daisies.

Daisy Wreath

Daisies are best made into fresh wreaths. Select mature blossoms and insert into a wet sphagnum moss base. A fern is a good companion to these living wreaths suggestive of youth and innocence.

Midsummer Day

Midsummer Day, which falls on June 24, is the celebration of the summer solstice, when the days are longest and the sun highest in the sky. In medieval times, it was considered a time of enchantment when fairies ran rampant in the meadows. It was also the time when marriageable girls were dressed in their finery and paraded before the eligible men. Maidens often wore chaplets composed of white lilies and vervain, and brides were crowned with roses.

Wedding Crown

Brides often wore wreaths as wedding crowns which were dried and passed down as heirlooms. Bridal wreaths can include ribbons, dried blossoms and fragrant herbs with special significance to the season or the bride. Roses were often used because they were associated with love and virtue.

St. Christopher's Day

St. Christopher's Day, celebrated on July 25, is a midsummer holiday of feasting and anticipation of the bounty of August. Because of the abundance of the season, there are many plants which were traditionally associated with this feast day. Among them are, baneberry, osmund fern, and wolves bane, to name just a few.

Herb and Spice Wreath

On a base of artemisia, fragrant herbs may be added in groups of wired bunches of three or four, so that they may be easily removed for use in the kitchen. Attach a ring of bay and in the center, nutmegs, cinnamon and cardamom. Finally, add herbs of significance to you or those you use frequently in the kitchen: caraway, anise, coriander or rue can be tied to the wreath under a velvet bow.

Lammas Day

Lammas Day, August 1, marks the beginning of the harvest season. It was originally a day of worship for the Roman deity Ceres, goddess of the harvest. The first grains of the season were baked into bread on this day, as an offering of thanksgiving. Later, in Christian times, the first fruits of the field were offered to the church.

Wheat is most commonly associated with this holiday.

Lammas Day Wreath

Italian bearded wheat makes an excellent Lammas Day wreath. Attach sheaves to a base of artemisia and decorate with dried calendulas. This wreath makes a delightful front door ornament.

Michaelmas

This harvest festival is celebrated on September 29. This is the height of the drying season. In agrarian times, this was a feast to give thanks for the fruit of the fields. It was also an enchanted time, when townsfolk hung yew, bracken, and other pungent herbs to ward off witchcraft and keep the hearths of home safe as the days grew shorter and winter made its first approach.

Incense Wreath

The most fragrant of wreaths, the incense wreath contains the must unusual materials, and glows with warm autumn colors. On a base of artemisia and sweet grass we add tonka beans, cinnamon sticks and small pieces of sweet smelling sandalwood. To complete the design, we attach a bow and tie in two small bags of frankincense and myrrh. These can easily be removed and burned as incense.

All Hallow's Eve.

All Hallow's Eve falls on October 31, on the eve of All Saint's Day. Historically, All Hallow's Eve was an enchanted time when witches and goblins ruled the night. Witch's wreaths composed of fragrant herbs known for their ability to discourage spirit tricksters, were hung from the rafters, and over thresholds to protect the families within.

Witch's Wreath

The witch's wreath represents the many plants that both attract and repel witchcraft. Some essential plants to use are rue, wild geranium, willow, hawthorne, elder, alder, and rowan tree berries. Oak leaves and vervain were also believed to hinder the witch. Rowan berries add color and extra interest.

St. Martin's Day

St. Martin's Day, falling on November 11, marks the beginning of the Advent season. In Northern Europe, the great Christmas market opens on this day. Traditionally, it was also the time of year that farmers slaughtered their livestock, and salted the winter meat. Feasting, therefore, and fond farewells as workers left for homes or winter jobs, ruled the day.

St. Martin's Day Wreath

A good St. Martin's wreath is a circle of braided straw wrapped with cheerful, embroidered woven binding. Sprigs of boxwood give a festive, holiday look. Lady apples can be wired into the base for color, as they are symbolic of the harvest. A bright bow accented with a sprig of boxwood completes the wreath.

St. Nicholas' Day

St, Nicholas' day is a holiday for those with a sweet tooth. Beautiful cookie molds are used for the famous springerle, or anise cake and baked goods abound. Traditionally, yellow blossoms, such as yarrow or tansy, representing the famous bags of gold that this Dutch saint distributed to the poor, were symbolic of the holiday, and Dutch children would find gold pieces in their shoes on Christmas morning.

St. Nicholas' Wreath

A St. Nicholas' wreath may be made with evergreens or artemisia as a base. Sweet Annie is an appropriate choice, because its gold color is symbolic of the day. You can find cookie molds in a variety of interesting shapes, which make fine decorations for this wreath. To finish, wire bunches of cinnamon sticks and nutmeg, or other spices commonly used to flavor holiday treats.

Harvest and Preservation

The best time to pick material for wreath making is late morning, when the dew has dried but the sun has not yet bleached out colors and essential oils. Flower color is brightest when blossoms first open. Many flowers will continue opening after they have been cut, so watch them closely and cut blooms when they are fully formed.

Heavy stemmed plants, such as willow, bitter sweet or grapevine should be stripped of leaves as soon as they are picked and formed immediately into wreath bases while they are still pliable.

Many herbs can be dried by hanging in bunches. If you won't be using the leaves, strip them from the stems. As plants dry, the stems shrivel and may have to be re-tied. Keep them protected from moisture and light.

Large stems that will be used for wreath bases are best dried in baskets. The stems of artemisia dry into gently curling shapes when dried in this fashion, and are much easier to form into wreaths.

Rosebuds and other flowers that will be wired dry well in a single layer on trays or screens. Place these screens away from light in an airy spot. Decorative seed pods harvested from the garden or the fields can also be dried in this manner.

Many flowers dry best when placed in a drying medium, such as sand, borax, or silica gel. If you choose to use sand, first wash it until it is perfectly clean and dry it thoroughly. Spread a think layer of medium over the bottom of a wide, shallow container. Place the flowers in the powder so that the blossoms don't touch. Gently pour the drying medium over and around the flowers until they are completely buried. Leave the containers to stand in a warm dry room and lift dried flowers carefully from medium once they are dry. Use a soft brush to clean away remaining granules.

Certain plants do not dry well and need to be treated with a preservative. Infusing a glycerin solution into leaves and berries preserves their natural color and texture.

Making a Wreath Base

To construct an artemisia base, use stems of silver king with the curling tops removed. Begin by bending the stems evenly around the wire frame, securing them together with wire as you go. Do not wire them too tightly. You will need room to insert springs of the silver tips into the base. Cover the back of the base with strands of artemisia to give it a finished look.

When you are satisfied with your base, begin to cover it by inserting the feather tips of the artemisia branches. You may use individual sprays or prepared bundles. Turn the curls toward the center, working clockwise until the circle is filled. Shape the outside line carefully as you work in order to maintain a good circle. Control stragglers by wrapping wire lightly around the whole wreath and then covering the wire with more artemisia sprays.

Decorating

After the base is completed, you are ready to add decorative material. If you are using weak stemmed flowers, wire them before inserting them into your wreath with lightweight florist's wire. Gently but firmly push the end of the wire into the base of the bloom; hold the base of the bloom in one hand, and gradually twist the wire around the stem of the flower; then it is ready to insert into the wreath base. Push your wired or stiff stemmed flower firmly into the base.

If you are using spices, they need to be pierced and wired. Use a small bit to drill holes in nutmeg and cinnamon; then wire them together in bunches of three with florist's wire. Cardamom can be pierced with a sturdy needle or stiff wire.

To add little bags of spices or potpourri, twist them closed with fine wire and attach them under the bow of the wreath. To make a hangar for your wreath, twist a piece of wire to form a small loop in the center. Then work the ends of the wire into the framework of the wreath to secure them.

Living Wreath

A living wreath is made on a special wire frame which must be packed with sphagnum moss and soaked thoroughly with water. Then begin inserting plants.

Living wreaths must be put on trays to hold moisture and to make watering possible. If kept moist, a living wreath lasts almost indefinitely. Water the moss at least once a week.

Making Garlands

To make a garland, start by braiding together wild flowers, such as daisies, with ferns and grasses. Insert clusters of clovers and daisies into each strand; they will create a lovely background for other flowers you may wish to add.

You may also bind a few stems of flowers or grasses together with fine wire. Knot the wire firmly around the stems, take several turns around the length of the stems, and finish with a knot, but do not cut the wire. Position a second bunch of flowers over the stems of the first and continue, first tying a knot, then wrapping the stems, this time joining the stems of both bunches. Secure it with a knot before adding a third bunch. Proceed until the flower rope is of desired length.

Tools and Supplies

WIRE FRAMES: Wire rings are readily available and inexpensive, so we suggest purchasing rather than making one. When you are choosing your ring size, bear in mind that to the frame dimension, you will add two or three inches of material. For living wreaths, you will need a wire frame made with four concentric circles of wire cross-braced with wire so that they have some height or depth. Ten-inch frames or larger work best.

WIRE: of various weights and types is an absolute necessity. You will need green-coated, florist's's wire for binding evergreens, and silver wire for artemisia and statice.

WIRE CUTTER AND STEM CUTTER, may be combined in a single tool if you can find one. The one we use at Caprilands was originally an electrician's tool and works efficiently for both purposes.

A GLUE GUN is helpful when you need to place small, unruly bits into a design.

AN ELECTRIC DRILL is necessary for whole spices and these materials must be drilled before being attached to the wreath.